Wounds and wisdom

Amanda Morrison

BookLeaf
Publishing

India | USA | UK

Wounds and wisdom © 2024 Amanda Morrison

All rights reserved.

No part of this publication may be reproduced, stored in a retrieval system, or transmitted, in any form or by any means, electronic, mechanical, photocopying, recording or otherwise, without the prior written permission of the presenters.

Amanda Morrison asserts the moral right to be identified as author of this work.

Presentation by *BookLeaf Publishing*

Web: www.bookleafpub.com

E-mail: info@bookleafpub.com

ISBN: 9789360940898

First edition 2024

To anyone who has ever felt like they didn't belong, this is for you. My light is on, follow it home.

And to E..thank you for inspiring me. When it comes to you I have no words to describe what you mean to me.

Strange moon

Sit with me under the full moons light
Let's share this moment in the dead of night
When the world is asleep so peaceful and still
My heart can be yours and the stars to fill
And we can fill yours in a simple exchange
Is it supposed to feel this strange?
Butterflies dance in my stomach out of tune
I haven't a clue what they want me to do
I run in these circles all day long in my head
Do I spill to you my soul or do I stay silent
instead
Thinking of you makes my sky a little less gray
You're more than enough light to keep the
monsters at bay
So sit with me under a full moon's light
Don't speak a word just hold me tight

Whisper

When I look into your eyes
I lose all track of time
I just want to swim in those golden pools of
honey
A luxury you can surely not buy with money
I forgot we were talking for a moment
I was thinking of my heart and how you own it
You can have it all just say the word
But that's nothing you've never heard
Look into my eyes and tell me what you feel
Is this a cruel dream or could it be real?
We'll never know because we'll never try
No matter how much it makes me cry
I'll still love you all the same
Even if I never hear you whisper my name

Remember me

Remember me
The person you never wanted to be
I see you looking at me in the mirror
Your vision is blurry but mine is getting clearer
You're breaking your promises again
Fighting demons and they're starting to win
I try to yell but you won't listen
My warnings you seem to be missing
You swore you would never be me
Never compromise on your beliefs
You're slacking and it shows
Unwatered plants never grow
It's not too late there's still time
Long as you listen to this message of mine
Change while you have the chance
Or get caught in the devil's dance
Look in the mirror and what do you see
Is this the person you wanted to be

Tuesday

I once tried to end my life
Acting like it was an ordinary Tuesday night
I know it's hard to believe
But the truth is what lies underneath
That's because you only see my smile
Not knowing I've been faking it all the while
There's this crushing weight heavy on my soul
And sometimes I feel it just swallows me whole
You would know if you looked deep into my
eyes
That I'm suffocating behind these walls of mine
I yell for help but nobody is there
Maybe they can't hear me through all the despair
I feel like I'm slipping into insanity
Been killing myself for years death has become
a part of my reality
I struggle with these voices screaming in my
head
Telling me I'm worthless and I'm better off dead
But I lied and told you I was fine
This pain was no one else's it was only mine
Then one Tuesday when I was about to give in
Was where my life decided to begin
These words started flowing out of me like an
endless sea

And suddenly not even I could stop me
I thought it was my darkest night
So the universe sparked my light
Now it shines everywhere that I go
Beautiful broken pieces, a kaleidoscope of soul
Hold on for one more day
I can promise you help is on the way

Go ahead, stop me

I'm no longer asking for permission or
forgiveness
You're going to get what you get
And you're going to take it
I'll shower you with affection like a raging storm
You can hide under that umbrella all you want
You're still gonna get wet
You can bet against me sure go ahead
You'll have better luck when I'm dead
I can't stop now what was I thinking
I forgot I could swim I was too busy sinking
I got a stiff drink waiting in the shade
There are things to do and memories to be made
Places to see and people to love
There's always darkness creeping below
But there's also always light above
So love me hate me I care less either way
I'm choosing to love myself everyday
So I hope you like stormy weather

Friends, I promise

Let the sun kiss your cheek in my place
Feel its warmth like a soft embrace
Let the wind run through your hair
Like my fingers long to be there
If the sun is too much allow my shadow to be
your shade
I'll stay perfectly still until the sunlight fades
When the moon shines down on you at night
Just maybe you'll think of me and smile in
delight
I ask for nothing much in return
For my friendship you already earned

Walls

I see the crack in your walls
If they break much more they'll begin to fall
You try to repair the brick and mortar
Trying so desperately to hide your feelings like a
hoarder
You can't hide forever, you were never meant
too
Meant to be free as the sky is blue
I won't say a word, I didn't see a thing
Just like I pretend you're not the song I sing

Fate

They say you can't fight fate
But fate is just consequences for the choices we
make
Who is to say what song the Blackbird sings
Nonetheless it's melodies carry on the breeze
No one tells the sun when it can shine
So what's so different about this light of mine
They say it all happens for a reason
But their reasoning changes with the season
Maybe it was fate or just dumb luck
Long as you don't, I don't give a fuck

Gifts

It's a gift and a curse to feel so deep yet not at all
Broken time and time again I'm numb to the fall
But what's this light that has found me in the
dark
Shining on the broken pieces of my heart
It comes and goes of it's own free will
I hold back my tears but they begin to spill
Each teardrop makes the light seem brighter
And this heavy soul of mine feels a bit lighter
Then I feel too much and I'm afraid you'll fade
Just like all the lights that never stayed
I swatted them away like annoying pests
Then again you're different then the rest
Your light is always flickering reminding me
you're there
Some days you shine so bright it's hard not to
stare
I try not to think about you but I'm afraid that
order is too tall
It's a gift and a curse to feel so much yet nothing
at all

Shine

You are the stars and I just want to be your
mirror
I just want you to see yourself clearer
Look me in my eyes if you think I'm lying
See how they shine ever so blinding
They never are just words on a page to read
But an oath I'll forever keep
If you shine on me, I'll shine on you
No words could ever be more true

Ocean

I've traveled through the darkness
Like a small boat being tossed about in the
ocean
Holding on to the hope of making shore
Fighting to keep afloat
Suddenly the dark menacing clouds part
Breathtaking stars now shining down
Showing me a glimpse of the heavens
There is one star that is the brightest in the sky
Calling my name in soft whispers
I can't help but to chase after it
Like a moth to a flame

Spring

Its spring time
You can smell the scent of fresh rain in the air
Intoxicating to the soul
you feel the moisture hit your skin like
microscopic kisses
The rumble of thunder growing in the distance
as the clouds and wind sway and swirl like
dancing lovers across the sky
Hoping the clouds will clear for a crystal clear
night of dazzling stars and moonlight
With some sun and a bit of luck
Some flowers will bloom from the smallest
seeds
Ah yes it's spring time indeed

Hug

Let me hug you just a moment longer
While your thoughts start to wander
I want to memorize every detail while I can
We never know when we'll get the chance again
I want you to feel safe with my arms wrapped
around tight
The only inches between us being our height
Seems by the day I just grow fonder
Let me hug you just a moment longer

Follow me

Follow me with your weary soul
If you want my hand is there to hold
You can rest if you need if only for awhile
I can guide you out of the menacing wilds
Let me be the light like you were for me
I'll show you the most beautiful sky you've ever
seen
You can put that weight down, it looks heavy to
hold
Then again you'll never carry it alone
I'll be there when the night seems lonely and
cold
To tell you to follow me with your weary soul

I thought I saw you

I thought I saw you yesterday
Standing in a crowd as I walked by
But I knew it was only a trick of the eye
Or was it a stab from the heart?
I have only counted the days since we've been
apart

I thought I saw you again today
Watching me from the doorway
I go to call out your name
Sadly only silence came

I know you are following me
That's three times this week
I know I need to visit more often
But it was hard enough to see you in that coffin

I guess you are staying with me
Hiding in the shadows playfully
Even when I visit to lay flowers down
But you always were my favorite clown

Maybe

Maybe we have met each other before
Somewhere on a distant sandy shore
In another time or perhaps a past life
Maybe it's gray and not so black and white
I have this dream where we finally meet
But it's not a stranger that I've come to greet
Your eyes feel more like a memory when they
look in mine
Maybe we met before in a different time

Welcome to my life

Welcome to my life
I say good morning when clearly it's night
And whisper good night in the morning light
When the world is busy doing
I'm sprawled out in bed peacefully snoozing
Just as I begin to wake
The twilight sky starts to break
The moon is my sun as it playfully shines
Reflecting in these star struck eyes of mine
I'm just a creature of the night
Romantic like studying you by candlelight
I smile at the stars with wonder in my heart
Are you too staring in the dark
As the world sleeps and the chaos slacks
I work hard and bust my back
Then once again I'm confused if it's morning or
night
But hey welcome to my life

You

I've seen the sun rise a thousand times
None of them compare to the shine in your eyes
I've danced to a million and one lovely songs
Yet my rhythm never seemed to belonged
Then you came along with the most beautiful
sound
And it sang to me til my heart it found
I have wished upon a many of stars
I wonder if they're brighter wherever you are

Evil queen

Oh honey I'm not the princess, I'm the evil queen
I don't want love songs I'd rather hear you
scream
There's nothing to fix because nothing is broken
Just a dark reflection of words fools have spoken
They call me a freak as if i should be surprised
Then again you get tiny thoughts from narrow
minds
They fear what they don't understand
Fear and mockery go hand in hand
Let them be fools who do all the saving
I'll be evil queen menacingly laughing

I lied

I may have stretched the truth
When I say it's just a crush on you
You run across my thoughts all the time
Feeling like I'm losing my damn mind
No matter what you're always there
My dearest friend with raven hair
How I wish you could feel the same
Maybe then I could be sane
Or we could be mad together
We could fly high if only we had feathers
I can't this madness anymore if I tried
When I said it's just a crush, I think I lied

www.ingramcontent.com/pod-product-compliance
Lightning Source LLC
Chambersburg PA
CBHW071255140726
47996CB00007B/2856